PERFECTLY FLAWED:
YOUR 30-DAY DEVOTIONAL GUIDE ON
HOW TO ACCEPT AND LOVE YOU

SEEING YOU THROUGH HIS EYES

BY SAMARIA KELLY

Perfectly Flawed: Your 30-Day Devotional Guide on
How to Accept and Love You – Seeing You Through His
Eyes

Subscribe to www.samariakelly.com for more
inspirational products.

Perfectly Flawed: Your 30-Day Devotional Guide on How to Accept and Love You — Seeing You Through His Eyes

True Victory Media
8110 Creekbend Drive Houston, TX 77071
www.TruVictoryentertainment.com

ISBN: 978-1-7370153-0-7

Subscribe to www.samariakelly.com for more inspirational products.

Perfectly Flawed: Your 30-Day Devotional Guide on How to Accept and Love You – Seeing You Through His Eyes

Printed in The United States of America

Subscribe to www.samariakelly.com for more inspirational products.

Perfectly Flawed: Your 30-Day Devotional Guide on How to Accept and Love You – Seeing You Through His Eyes

Table of Contents

Subscribe to www.samariakelly.com for more inspirational products.

Perfectly Flawed: Your 30-Day Devotional Guide on How to Accept and Love You – Seeing You Through His Eyes

Subscribe to www.samariakelly.com for more inspirational products.

Subscribe to www.samariakelly.com for more inspirational products.

Perfectly Flawed: Your 30-Day Devotional Guide on How to Accept and Love You – Seeing You Through His Eyes

Subscribe to www.samariakelly.com for more inspirational products.

Perfectly Flawed: Your 30-Day Devotional Guide on How to Accept and Love You – Seeing You Through His Eyes

So do not throw away your confidence; it will be richly rewarded. You need to persevere so that when you have done the will of God, you will receive what He has promised. Hebrews 10:35-36 (NIV)

Perfectly Flawed: Your 30-Day Devotional Guide on How to Accept and Love You – Seeing You Through His Eyes

Subscribe to www.samariakelly.com for more inspirational products.

INTRODUCTION

Hey you, you are so beautiful and brave. I am so proud of you for deciding to embark on this journey with me. For a long time, self-doubt and insecurities hindered me from achieving my dreams and walking in my divine calling. As a child, I experienced years of sexual abuse, which caused me many emotional scars that damaged my self-confidence and self-esteem. As a result, I suffered many failed relationships and friendships. You could say I was an expert in acting because I hid my pain well and my bubbly personality made it easy for me to cover up my tears with laughter. That is why you should never judge a book by its cover.

I was screaming for help on the inside. I was active in church and always felt God around me, but I did not develop a personal relationship with Him until I was 18 years old. This is when the healing process for me began. It took me 30 years to even mention my trauma in any form publicly.

I knew I had to get over myself in order to be everything God has called me to be. I knew my pain would be used for a purpose, and I had to be intentional and let go to help others. This required me to spend time with Him and study His word to understand who I am and from who I come. Writing this devotional is my proof of growth, and I want to provide a source of freedom for anyone held captive to self-doubt or their insecurities. These 30 devotions will give you access to God's Word and truth on how to accept and love you by seeing you as He does.

These messages will change your perception, renew your mind, and draw you closer to Him. It's time to regain your power and accept that you are perfectly flawed and exactly the way God wants you to be. You will no longer aim to compromise who you are to fit in to what others or society deem as acceptable. There is nobody in the world exactly like you. He designed each one of us according to His perfect plan.

God gave us His word, which gives us strength in times of defeat. He knew that in this journey of life we will encounter many challenges because this world does not love us. His love is genuine, everlasting, and unconditional. Once you understand God's love, you will understand love and how to love.

Subscribe to www.samariakelly.com for more inspirational products.

Perfectly Flawed: Your 30-Day Devotional Guide on How to Accept and Love You – Seeing You Through His Eyes

Now is the time to invite Him into your heart, open your mind, remove every distraction, and receive the truth. We all know change is always intimidating in the beginning, especially when you have believed a lie for so long. It will require some soul searching. Eventually, with endurance, consistency, and application, you will feel relief and become victorious. Come along with me, this is your time of redemption.

Perfectly Flawed: Your 30-Day Devotional Guide on
How to Accept and Love You – Seeing You Through His
Eyes

DAY ONE
GOD CHOSE YOU

. . - - - - ● ● ● ◉ ◎ ◉ ● ● ● ● - - - . .

*This is the book of the generations of Adam. When
God created man, he made him in the likeness of
God. Male and female; he created them, and he
blessed them and named them Man when they were
created.* Genesis 5:1-2 (ESV)

We all have asked, why am I here? Or what is my purpose? I'm positive those questions come across our minds all the time, especially during times of failure or rejection. God wanted us here and designed us to reflect Him in the way we walk, talk, act, and treat each other. He made no errors in making us. We are not here by accident. What should stand out in this scripture the most is that immediately after He created us He blessed us. Blessed is defined as being used for expressing happiness or satisfaction. Holy and loved by God. We satisfied Him, and He saw that what He created was pleasant and gave us a name.

Perfectly Flawed: Your 30-Day Devotional Guide on How to Accept and Love You — Seeing You Through His Eyes

We are what He says we are, amen. We must constantly remind ourselves who we are and from who we come. This is a daily reassurance. Studying His Word is an appropriate starting point. This is how I built my strength and power. It definitely woke me up, and in order to stay awake, I had to choose Him often. This is the reason I favor the famous quote by Lewis Carroll from *Alice in Wonderland*: "I knew who I was this morning, but I changed a few times since then." It reminds me of how easily we can become vulnerable to the enemy and his lies if we let down our guards.

- Are you confident you are here for a purpose and chosen from greatness for greatness?
- If not, what is it going to require for you to align yourself with the Father?
- What are your exact convictions?

_____

_____

Dear Lord, I thank you for who you are and for giving me the breath of life. Thank you for seeing that I was good and pleasing. Continue to direct my path and help me see myself for who I am. In Jesus' Name, Amen.

Perfectly Flawed: Your 30-Day Devotional Guide on How to Accept and Love You – Seeing You Through His Eyes

DAY TWO
A WORK OF ART

- - - - ⁃ ⁃ ⁃ ⁃ ⁃ ⁜ ⁜ ⁜ ⁜ ⁜ ⁜ ⁜ ⁃ ⁃ ⁃ ⁃ ⁃ - - - -

For we are God's masterpiece, created in the Messiah Jesus to perform good actions that God prepared long ago to be our way of life. Ephesians 2:10 (ISV)

I cannot help but focus on that word: Masterpiece; it's defined as a work of outstanding artistry, skill, workmanship, or a "great literary masterpiece." We are to God as our favorite painting or picture on our wall in our living room is to us. Although, the beauty, dedication, and effort that flows from that piece is no comparison to us, even our most precious jewel has no parallel value. What comes to mind when you think of a masterpiece? I think of something that you would handle with profound love and attention. An object of extreme worth. I had to meditate on this scripture for a while. My friend, those things we see as defects in our distinction are actually reflections of

His outstanding creative ability. We are beyond extraordinary.

God gave us certain characteristics to set us apart from the rest. He has given each of us special gifts that He arranged for us long before we made our entrance to this world. These gifts are remarkable, or He wouldn't have said so. Jesus is the example of how we should execute our gifts through our daily walk.

- Do you believe He equipped you with the ability to produce good works?
- Do you feel like a walking masterpiece?
- Are you walking in authority and in His divine will?
- What is it going to require for you to present yourself as holy and acceptable?

_____

_____

Dear God, I magnify your name. I am your masterpiece. Your works are wonderful, and I adore you. I trust in you, and I know I am here on purpose for a purpose. Continue to lead me on the path of righteousness. In Jesus' Name, Amen.

Subscribe to www.samariakelly.com for more inspirational products.

Perfectly Flawed: Your 30-Day Devotional Guide on How to Accept and Love You – Seeing You Through His Eyes

DAY THREE
POWER UP

· · - - - ∘ ∘ ⊚ ⊚ ⊚ ⊛ ⊛ ⊛ ⊛ ⊛ ⊛ ⊚ ⊚ ∞ ∞ ∞ - · · · ·

Though an army besiege me, my heart will not fear; though war break out against me, even then I will be confident. Psalm 27:3 (NIV)

I wish I had this much God-inspired confidence back in the day. Although, even if I had of understood this verse, I probably wouldn't have appreciated this verse like I do now. It was about 20 years ago, in my early teens, when all those harsh words that were spoken toward me destroyed my self-esteem. Yeah, the boys took advantage of my well-developed shape and were not very nice with their words . . . I'm glad I know now I can depend on God, who is my source of power and strength when everything around me seems to be attacking me.

It does not matter what anyone has to say about me. It doesn't matter what traps the enemy sets in my path. My life could even fall into shambles, but because my confidence is not from me but from the One who created me, I am unstoppable. I can overcome any obstacles regardless of what I may believe or what I am facing.

I will not be afraid to try, even if failing is the outcome. I can face adversity and take chances and not regret them because I have a steady flow of strength and energy that will never end. This also reminds me of another scripture in His word when He told us to bring all of our worries, burdens, and stresses to Him, and He will give us rest. Mathew 11:28 (ESV) says, "Come to me, all who labor and are heavy laden, and I will give you rest." What a great relief! We don't have to fight alone, He will do it for us, which makes us automatic winners.

- How does this resonate with you?
- Do you understand who gives you your confidence and where you get your strength from in time of adversity?

_____

_____

Dear Lord, there is nothing I can't do because all my strength comes from you. Thank you for being my source of power and strength. In Jesus' name, Amen.

Subscribe to www.samariakelly.com for more inspirational products.

Perfectly Flawed: Your 30-Day Devotional Guide on How to Accept and Love You – Seeing You Through His Eyes

DAY FOUR
WONDERFULLY FORMED

- - - - - - - - ● ● ● ● ● ● ● ● ● ● ● - - - - - - - - -

For you formed my inward parts; you knitted me together in my mother's womb. I praise you, for I am fearfully and wonderfully made. Wonderful are your works; my soul knows it very well. Psalms 139:13-14 (ESV)

This is an affirmation for me. This gave me my confidence. This is for all of us suffering from insecurities, especially pertaining to body image. It saved me from self-destruction when I was battling depression over low self-esteem. In this we are acknowledging who we come from; we are showing confidence and admiration in our Creator. There is no lack of gratitude at this moment. We are positive He made us wonderful. God was detailed, careful, and specific with every piece of us.

Does that make your soul leap for joy? Mine has! I'm embarrassed to admit this to you, but I often complained to God about aspects of myself. Now I think: Some nerve of me. God doesn't need me to audit His work like He does not know what He is doing.

God is the Superior of design and creativity. There is no hand, mind, eye, or being who will ever compare to Him. His skill is beyond the human's brain. We are incapable of registering His artistry, so being included in the chosen speaks volumes. We are nothing short of amazing!

- Are you confident that He made you wonderful?
- What are your current struggles on this matter?
- What steps are necessary for you to take to gain the security you need within yourself?

Dear God, I humbly come to you, asking you to remove any thoughts and feelings of unworthiness from me. My faith is in you, and I know I am everything that you say that I am. You designed me, and I am wonderful because I came from you. I bless your holy name. In Jesus' name, Amen.

Subscribe to www.samariakelly.com for more
inspirational products.

Perfectly Flawed: Your 30-Day Devotional Guide on
How to Accept and Love You – Seeing You Through His
Eyes

DAY FIVE
UNDERSTAND FOR GOOD

He that getteth wisdom loveth his own soul; he that keepeth understanding shall find good. Proverbs 19:8 (KJV)

We often hear the phrase knowledge is power, but how effective is knowledge without understanding? We all have knowledge of love and self. By that I mean we know they exist, but that does not mean we understand them. This knowledge of love and self should just come naturally, but that is not the case for everyone. Many factors can alter our perception, such as trauma or betrayal.

This verse encourages us to love ourselves enough to *want* to discover the truth, despite where we are, and to receive it with gladness. Then if we continue to apply what we have learned, we will benefit from the fruitful things of life. We will be prosperous.

I know the moment I sought first the kingdom of heaven is when things started making sense and going in my favor. Matthew 6:33 says, "Seek ye first the kingdom of God and His righteousness; and all these things shall be added unto you." This means seek to spend time with God, listen and obey Him, and live a life modeled after Christ's. When you do, He will take care of everything else in your life for you. Always consult with God first when looking for direction or solutions to life's many challenges.

- Have you chosen God as your primary consultant?
- Are you using His word as your instruction manual?

_____

_____

Dear Heavenly Father, I know you are the Head of my life and if I continue to seek you first and foremost and in all things, I will gain wisdom that will allow me to receive all that you have for me. Everything I need is in you. Thank you for the love and peace that surpasses all understanding. In Jesus' name, Amen.

Perfectly Flawed: Your 30-Day Devotional Guide on
How to Accept and Love You – Seeing You Through His
Eyes

Subscribe to www.samariakelly.com for more
inspirational products.

DAY SIX
GOODBYE FEAR

- - - - - - - - - ● ● ● ● ● ● ● ● ● ● ● - - - - - - -

*For God gave us a spirit not of fear but of power
and love and self-control.* 2 Timothy 1:7 (ESV)

The Lord knows what we are capable of. He knows exactly what is within our scope of practice. He developed everything within us. He is certain of how we operate and what he placed inside of the operation. He gave us power over those things we believe we can't do. Fear is an unpleasant emotion caused by the belief that someone or something is dangerous, likely to cause pain, or a threat. It is something we have control over but allow to creep in anyway.

I remember the first time I had to sing in front of a large crowd. I was so nervous and scared that both of my legs were shaking. I had to control myself by imagining everybody in the crowd with bald heads and by looking slightly above the audience during the whole performance. This allowed me to make it through the performance

Subscribe to www.samariakelly.com for more
inspirational products.

without passing out. However, I could have overcome my fears in that very moment. God never created fear. It comes when we are the most vulnerable and when we are in situations where we are unsure of who we are or who has control over our lives.

Usually, this fear happens when we have given some or all of our power over to someone or something. For example, a wife who stays in an abusive relationship will always have fear until she leaves the abuse. The moment she stayed, she gave her power over to her husband. Or the man who lost his job and drank his loss away. He lost self-control because he was unsure of when his next check was coming. He picked up alcohol rather than using his power to say, "That's ok. I will put on my suit and tie tomorrow and apply for another job."

The enemy has a field day when we allow fear to control us, but God has given us power over all things. We must believe in ourselves, believe in the one who chose us, and stand firm on His word. Only then will we be able to overcome fear.

- Are you allowing fear to keep coming into your life?
- If so, how can you defeat it?

Perfectly Flawed: Your 30-Day Devotional Guide on How to Accept and Love You – Seeing You Through His Eyes

- Do you understand the gifts God has given you?

_____

_____

Dear Heavenly Father, you have complete control over my life. I know that you have not given me a spirit of fear; it has no place in my heart. You made me a winner and have given me dominion and power over the enemy. I can do all things through Christ who strengthens me. In Jesus' name, Amen.

Subscribe to www.samariakelly.com for more inspirational products.

Perfectly Flawed: Your 30-Day Devotional Guide on How to Accept and Love You – Seeing You Through His Eyes

Subscribe to www.samariakelly.com for more inspirational products.

DAY SEVEN
BE ENCOURAGED

Have I not commanded you? Be strong and courageous. Do not be afraid; do not be discouraged, for the Lord your God will be with you wherever you go. Joshua 1:9 (NIV)

This speaks to the perfectionist in me. I would waste so much time analyzing everything I created to put in front of someone because I was afraid of embarrassment, afraid that someone would not like my truth, or afraid that my truth just wasn't up to standard. But whose standards was I trying to meet in the first place? That's the question I had to ask myself in order to free myself from bondage. It was like I was having a wrestling match with myself.

God will never leave us or forsake us. He is with us in every situation. When we feel inadequate or not at our best, he is there to strengthen us. We are perfect only through him; we cannot do anything without his permission. That is why our weaknesses are not failures. They are opportunities that allow God to use his power and teach us it is ok to mess up; it is ok to not have it all; and it is okay to have malfunctions. This should give us enough courage and motivation to just go for it--whatever it is we have been afraid of doing. God is always with us.

- What is holding you back from achieving your dreams?
- When did the security breach happen in your life?
- How can you push past it?

_____

_____

Dear Lord, thank you for giving me the courage to fight through my challenges. I know I can overcome my fears because you are with me always. In Jesus' name, amen.

Perfectly Flawed: Your 30-Day Devotional Guide on
How to Accept and Love You – Seeing You Through His
Eyes

Subscribe to www.samariakelly.com for more
inspirational products.

DAY EIGHT
IT'S LOVE OR NOTHING AT ALL

- - - · · · · ● ● ● ● ● ● ● ● ● ● ● ● ● · · · · · ·

*If I speak in the tongues of men and angels but have
not love, I am a noisy gong or a clanging cymbal.
And if I have prophetic powers, and understand all
mysteries and all knowledge, and if I have all faith,
so as to remove mountains, but have not love, I am
nothing. If I give away all I have, and if I deliver up
my body to be burned, but have not love, I gain
nothing.* 1 Corinthians 13:1-3 (ESV)

Love wins over every single thing--no
matter what that thing is, no matter how great it is,
how rich it is, how popular. If love is not present,
the thing has no value. It is nonexistent. We can
have the greatest voice, the best dance skills, a
giving heart, we can even give up our lives, but it
does not mean a thing to God if love is absent.

Thinking deeply about this, I realized that, if
only there were way more emphasis and
conversation about love in the church, as explained
in this scripture, so much more love would be

present in our world. Our churches should focus on this message of love instead of messages of prosperity, health, or riches (which are promises of God but are not His priority). In fact, love will open the doors to all these things and also resolve many of the issues of the heart of people. Love must come first.

God says in this passage that we can speak in tongues and preach the gospel, even teach it well, but if it is without love, we are just making a loud noise and what we are proclaiming is not being heard but hurting someone's ears. He even said that we can have prophetic powers and wisdom with faith, but without love, it is all useless.

- Are you truly representing God's love in your life?
- Are there any changes that must take place in order for you to be effective?

_____

_____

Dear God, let my works not be in vain. Let love shine through my every act. Continue to order my steps, Oh Lord. May my life reflect your goodness and love. In Jesus' name, Amen.

Subscribe to www.samariakelly.com for more inspirational products.

Perfectly Flawed: Your 30-Day Devotional Guide on How to Accept and Love You – Seeing You Through His Eyes

DAY NINE
UPHELD BY HIM

- - - - - - - - - - ● ● ● ● ● ● ● ● ● ● ● ● - - - - - - - -

*So do not fear, for I am with you; do not be
dismayed, for I am your God. I will strengthen you
and help you; I will uphold you with my righteous
right hand.*
Isaiah 41:10 (ESV)

God is like, "Look, I got your back! I am
your Father! I will not let anybody count you out.
Let me handle those things that seem impossible or
too heavy for you to carry alone. I got you
covered!" This verse reminds me of when I am
trying to fix everything. I sometimes think I'm
superwoman, but it is impossible for me to carry the
weight of the entire world on my shoulders. We
have to have realistic expectations for ourselves.

God is relieving the pressure on us by
carrying our burdens for us. We don't have to be
there for everybody; we don't have to do
everything. Relax and let go of your anxiety, free
your worries, and allow God to do His job. There is

nothing too hard for Him. He knows exactly what He is doing. He will give you strength and guide you with His right hand. Will you trust Him?

- Where do you receive your help and strength?
- On whom do you depend?

_____

_____

Dear Heavenly Father, thank you for always being available to me. I know you will never leave me nor forsake me. All my help and strength comes from you; therefore, I will not be afraid. In Jesus' name, Amen.

Perfectly Flawed: Your 30-Day Devotional Guide on
How to Accept and Love You — Seeing You Through His
Eyes

Subscribe to www.samariakelly.com for more
inspirational products.

DAY TEN
LOVE PERFECTED

There is no fear in love, but perfect love casts out fear. For fear has to do with punishment, and whoever fears they have not perfected in love. 1 John 4:18. (ESV)

Many times love has to fight to win because fear has lived in us for so long. When this happens, it hinders us from receiving all of God, who is perfect love. Perfect means complete and mature. So anyone who has perfect love makes fear irrelevant. Love does no wrong because it's correct in all its ways. Therefore, there are no consequences for which to be afraid.

I battled with this idea. It was hard for me to accept love because I had trust issues. I was afraid of allowing my heart to be vulnerable because of past trauma, and the reality for me was that my trust had to be in God and not man. Man will disappoint you, but God will never wrong you. Therefore, if I trust God, I trust love because God is love.

Subscribe to www.samariakelly.com for more inspirational products.

This realization elevated me to another level. My sleep is peaceful because I know God is my all. His love brings a calmness that is beyond this world. As we build our relationship with God and grow closer to him daily, love will automatically perfect itself. Stay with Him, and love stays. However, the moment we decide to leave him and redirect our focus onto this world, we become a target for fear.

- Are you living in fear?
- Have you truly mastered love?
- If not, what steps are necessary for you to take to perfect it?

_____

_____

Dear Lord, I come to you with a heart of readiness. I am ready to be perfected in love, but I need your help. I need you to give me the strength to overcome my fears. Only you can do this. I am allowing myself to let you have your way. In Jesus' name, Amen.

Perfectly Flawed: Your 30-Day Devotional Guide on How to Accept and Love You – Seeing You Through His Eyes

DAY ELEVEN
LOVE WINS OVER SINS

Wherefore I say unto thee, her sins, which are many, are forgiven; for she loved much: but to whom little is forgiven, the same loveth little. Luke 7:47 (KJV)

If we are not giving love out, we are receiving little pardon for our evil deeds, my friend. God is so passionate about his love that, even during many of our wrongdoings, mishaps, and evil works, he will excuse us if we love much. If we continue to love ourselves and each other without conditions, we are acting as forgivers. God is telling us, if we can forgive much, he will show us mercy too, even though we are unworthy. He expects us to love more than do anything else. The emphasis in the New Testament is always on love above all. The reason for this is because if we love, it cancels out evil spontaneously.

Love will give us conviction and make us want to do what is right. This reminds me of another scripture in his word that states "love covers a multitude of sins." 1 Peter 4:8. In this verse, I picture Jesus on the cross. His love for us allowed him to lay his life down for all of our sins. He wants us to always remember how much he loves us, the importance of sharing his love with others, and the requirement that we forgive our fellow brothers and sisters as he forgave us out of his love for us.

- Is there no forgiveness in your heart?
- How does this resonate with you right now?
- How can you position yourself in right standing with God on this matter?

_____

_____

Dear God, I hope to please you. I want more of you so that my life can represent you well. Remove any unclean thing from me and give me peace with my brothers and sisters. Be my guide and director, Lord. In Jesus' name, Amen.

Perfectly Flawed: Your 30-Day Devotional Guide on
How to Accept and Love You – Seeing You Through His
Eyes

Subscribe to www.samariakelly.com for more
inspirational products.

Perfectly Flawed: Your 30-Day Devotional Guide on
How to Accept and Love You – Seeing You Through His
Eyes

DAY TWELVE
CHANGE YOUR MIND

- -

Do not be conformed to this world, but be transformed by the renewal of your mind, that by testing you may discern what is the will of God, what is good and acceptable and perfect. Romans 12:2 (ESV)

We are on this journey to grow and build a closer relationship with God. We cannot be doing what everyone else is doing around us. We cannot allow the world to distract us from the will of God. We must choose the path He wants us to take. Will we choose the road less traveled? Or will we allow tradition and what those who came before taught us keep us in our comfort zone?

Let us not fill up on fleshly desires and cause our spirit to die from hunger. It's ok to desire good things, but it should not be our focus. When we focus on God and walk with him daily, we will transform our thoughts, our actions, and our way of living. We will desire what he desires, dislike what

Subscribe to www.samariakelly.com for more inspirational products.

he dislikes, and only then will we understand his will and what is acceptable in his sight. This will allow us to fight temptation and survive through our tests and trials with our head held high because we know who we know and what we know!

We cannot be foolish and believe this world loves us more than our Father. It feels good when it seems like we are popular and accepted by society, but we are never truly happy and fulfilled because it is a false reality. It is a temporary distraction that separates us from our Father. Do not allow the world to deceive you. We are unique. He chose us to be peculiar people.

- Who do you look like? The world or Jesus?
- Are you walking with the right One in the right direction?
- If not, how can you get back on track?

_____

_____

Dear Lord, I know you have chosen me to be set apart from the world. I am also choosing you to be the map of my life and align my ways to be acceptable to you. I trust your perfect plan for me. Let your will be done in my life. In Jesus' name, Amen.

Subscribe to www.samariakelly.com for more inspirational products.

Perfectly Flawed: Your 30-Day Devotional Guide on How to Accept and Love You – Seeing You Through His Eyes

DAY THIRTEEN
TAILORED MADE

· · · · · · ● ● ● ● ● ● ● ● ● ● ● ● · · · · · · ·

Then God said, "Let us make man in our image, after our likeness. And let them have dominion over the fish of the sea and the birds of the heavens and the livestock and all the earth and over every creeping thing that creeps on the earth." Genesis 1:26 (ESV)

God put us at the top of His list of valuables. He created us to have authority and rank over all living and nonliving things. To have that much power is an honor. No money, silver, gold, diamond, precious gem, or fine jewelry has more value. We may wonder: How could one be so fond of us? What is it about us that makes him love us so? I have asked this question many times, and it is apparent that it is because we are a part of him. He made us in his likeness. We are his babies. I can see the excitement in his face when he made us.

It's like getting your first car, having your first child, or making your first good meal. It is a feeling that is that same excitement when we first achieve anything. That's the joy and confidence I'm envisioning God had when he prepared us. We matter so much to him that we cannot even measure it. It's indescribable. Just imagine love on steroids times infinity and beyond! Too powerful to even imagine.

- Do you feel worthy?
- Do you know how valuable you are?
- How can you view yourself in that same manner?

Dear Heavenly Father, I thank you for seeing the best in me. Thank you for showing me how worthy I am and of how much value I am. Please cleanse my mind and heart of doubt and guilt, and remove anything that is hindering me from moving forward and walking in authority. In Jesus' name, Amen.

Perfectly Flawed: Your 30-Day Devotional Guide on How to Accept and Love You – Seeing You Through His Eyes

Subscribe to www.samariakelly.com for more inspirational products.

DAY FOURTEEN
IN A DIFFERENT CLASS

. . . . ● ● ● ● ● ● ● ● ● ● ● ● . . . . . .

Not that we dare to classify or compare ourselves with some of those who are commending themselves. But when they measure themselves by one another and compare themselves with one another, they are without understanding. 2 Corinthians 10:12 (ESV)

We must not try to fit in to get in. We have to stop trying to look, sound, dress, and act like everybody who is popular by demand rather than The Man upstairs. Why do we strive so hard to be like those who are in a certain class or hold a particular title that gets them fame, fortune, or flattery? We cannot use them as a measure to calculate how good we are or how much value we have. We are different, and each individual has a specific gift and purpose for the kingdom of God.

The earth is full of distinguished individuals. We must trust our own awesomeness. We must be confident in what the Lord said about us and what he has awarded us. Those who commend themselves are without wisdom and are foolish. Every good thing is from the Lord, and it is him who gives us everything. No man does anything without the Lord allowing him. Those who are show-offs are blind and incapable of humbling themselves. God deserves all praise, honor, and glory. The only thing worth comparing ourselves to is God's standard for us in his Word.

- Are you being true to who he calls you to be?
- Are you standing out on your own, or do you look like everybody else?
- What is your exact conviction, and how can you come forward and away from it?

_____

_____

Dear God, I know you are the author and finisher of my faith, and that means my focus should be on you. I'm confident that everything in me is because of you, and you get all the glory. Nothing is possible without you. I thank you for who you are, and what you have chosen me to be. In Jesus' name, Amen.

Subscribe to www.samariakelly.com for more
inspirational products.

Perfectly Flawed: Your 30-Day Devotional Guide on How to Accept and Love You – Seeing You Through His Eyes

DAY FIFTEEN
UNBLEMISHED

· · · · - - - ● ● ● ● ● ● ● ● ● ● ● ● ● ● ● ● ● · · · - - - · ·

*Even as He chose us in Him before the foundation
of the world, that we should be holy and blameless
before Him in love.* Ephesians 1:4 (ESV)

God did not establish the world until he
found us in love first. He selected us to be holy and
without fault. We were instruments of complete
perfection and made to worship and praise our
Father in spirit and truth. Good deeds should be our
nature and not forced, meaning they should come
from the heart. This was God's intention, for it was
this way before anything came into existence. In
every effort and opportunity, we shall seek to
produce exceptional deeds. It behooves us to look to
Jesus as our example of a righteous life always.

The moment we feel like a situation or
person forces us to go left, think of Jesus and keep
right. That is our created nature. Remember the
popular phrase: What would Jesus do? (often
abbreviated W.W.J.D.). Keep this in the back of

your head and engraved on your hearts. It will motivate us to live by His principles as purposed.

However, he also gave us free will. Although we are to be of goodwill and live by it, we have to decide to walk in our divine purpose in order to fulfill it. Spend time with God in quiet and in his word, and he will show you the way he wants you to go.

- Are you producing good fruit?
- Are you doing what pleases God?
- What can you do to change your walk so that it aligns with God's will for your life?

_____

_____

Dear Lord, I humbly come to you asking you to make my crooked ways straight and let my daily walk be a journey of producing good fruits. Oh Lord, I pray that my labor here will store up my treasures in heaven. Let your will be done on earth as it is in Heaven. In Jesus' name, Amen.

Perfectly Flawed: Your 30-Day Devotional Guide on
How to Accept and Love You – Seeing You Through His
Eyes

DAY SIXTEEN
HIGHLY VALUED

- - - - - - - - - - ● ● ● ● ◆ ◆ ● ● ● ● - - - - - - -

Why, even the hairs of your head are all numbered. Fear not; you are of more value than many sparrows. Luke 12:7(ESV)

It's thought-provoking that he numbered the tiny hairs on our heads. That alone should bring much insight into how special we are to our Creator. To understand that magnitude of love and careful attention to detail is impeccable. Wow! This should make us feel untouchable, nothing should make us feel less than anything. Sparrows are peaceful, powerful small birds that bring charisma, so to have that comparison of having more significance than many of them speaks highly of us.

We can achieve anything we want to do. With this much power and worth, there is no way we can lose. He designed us for Victory. So where is all of this fear, doubt, and disbelief coming from inside us? It's unwarranted because nothing can change the fact that we are born Victors! As we gather our thoughts and prepare to journal them ask yourself:

- Do you feel important?
- Do you understand your value?
- If not, what challenges do you face and what is essential to overcome them?

_____

_____

Dear Lord, I thank you for who I am today. I praise you for loving me and seeing my worth even when I couldn't see it for myself. I know I matter because I come from you. Thank you for choosing me as a priority and for showing me grace and mercy when I am undeserving. Thank you for caring enough about me to number the hairs on my head. Give me the strength to overcome my fears and challenges through this process of learning my true worth in you. In Jesus' name, Amen.

Subscribe to www.samariakelly.com for more inspirational products.

Perfectly Flawed: Your 30-Day Devotional Guide on How to Accept and Love You – Seeing You Through His Eyes

Subscribe to www.samariakelly.com for more inspirational products.

DAY SEVENTEEN
A SPECIAL LOVE

- - - · · • • ⊕ ⊕ ⊕ ● ⊛ ⊛ ⊛ ● • • • · · · - -

*See what kind of love the Father has given to us,
that we should be called children of God; and so we
are. The reason why the world does not know us is
that it did not know him.* 1 John 3:1 (ESV)

It's difficult for us to grasp just how much
love God has for us. To be chosen and picked, to be
his heirs, to be a piece of him, it is a privilege and
honor. Nothing should be able to separate us from
him. Nothing and no-one should be able to
discourage us from anything. No wonder the world
doesn't agree with who we are. It could never love
this way, without conditions, without judgment,
without criticism. It will never know what it will
never accomplish. Since the world refuses to accept
God wholeheartedly and is completely ignorant to
him, it will never recognize our worth and who we
are.

When we look at poverty, child hunger,
suicide, murder, all of those tragic events, it is

imperative that we understand that this is not a God thing, like many are claiming. God is full of love, and he takes care of his own. (Now this does not mean He will not chastise us when we are disobedient, as there are consequences that result from poor decisions. Free will is something he gave us control over.) Our God is unfamiliar to this world, so His love is also foreign to it. This is clear by the absence of sufficient love and abundant calamity. We are not of this world.

- Who do you put your trust?
- Which side are you leaning on?
- Are you proud to be a child of The Most High God?
- Are you allowing shame to mask your truth?

Dear Lord, I may be in this world, but I am not of this world. I know my life is in your hands. Please continue to guide me through the valley of the shadow of death. I will not fear evil for I know you are with me always. I am yours and you are mine. Bless you, Oh God. In Jesus' name, Amen.

Subscribe to www.samariakelly.com for more inspirational products.

Perfectly Flawed: Your 30-Day Devotional Guide on
How to Accept and Love You – Seeing You Through His
Eyes

Subscribe to www.samariakelly.com for more
inspirational products.

DAY EIGHTEEN
OWN YOUR LIGHT

- - - - - - - - ● ● ● ● ● ● ● ● ● ● ● ● ● ● ● - - - - - -

You are the light of the world. A city set on a hill cannot be hidden. Nor do people light a lamp and put it under a basket but on a stand, and it gives light to all in the house. In the same way, let your light shine before others, so that they may see your good works and give glory to your father who is in heaven. Matthew 5:14-16 (ESV)

We are children of the light and should not be ashamed of who we are. By living and thriving, we are allowing God's glory to be revealed. As we promote righteousness loud and proud, this will intrigue others and cause even those who are strangers to be curious about us. As we continue to grow and align our ways with his, we will resemble him, and the old person will pass away and the new will take its rightful place. His light will forever shine.

We should never dim our lights to cover our authenticity but remain bold so others may see our example and also desire to glorify him. Improving and growing spiritually is a daily walk for all of us, and we strive to be who God has truly called us to be. We work toward excellence and perfection because He is perfect.

We are all facing challenges and will continue to go through tests and trials on this journey called life, but these trials are only there to strengthen our faith and prepare us for what is ahead. God's light will always prevail. As we continue to humble ourselves, upholding the truth and standing firm, we will continue to develop. In addition, as we are growing, glowing, and representing his glory, we will experience a consistent change that will eventually secure our name in his book, and that is the most important outcome of our walks.

- Are you letting his light shine?
- Are you representing him well and being true to who you are?
- Are you hiding behind a veil or are you up on a stand?
- What can you change to allow his light to shine through you?

Subscribe to www.samariakelly.com for more inspirational products.

Dear Heavenly Father, continue to shine your light on me and through me so that your mighty works and glory will be known to the world. Remove any stumbling block in my way. In Jesus' name, Amen.

Perfectly Flawed: Your 30-Day Devotional Guide on
How to Accept and Love You – Seeing You Through His
Eyes

DAY NINETEEN
BE A LOVE MAGNET

- -

Let not steadfast love and faithfulness forsake you; bind them around your neck; write them on the tablet of your heart. So you will find favor and success in the sight of God and man. Proverbs 3:3-4 (ESV)

Please stay trustworthy and remain honest and loyal. Keep love nested. Treat them as magnets, so they cannot go anywhere without being stuck to us. These are the core of treating others with the utmost respect and kindness. Do not let them escape, even when temptation arises and disappointment warrants. When we handle these fruits, our seeds will spring forth many blessings from God. The harvest will be abundant. The favor of the Lord will fall upon our lives. We will not experience many failures, and we will prosper.

This verse states that God will also bring us favor in the sight of our fellow man. People will start doing things for us without comprehending the reason behind it. We will not have to put much effort forth to show ourselves approved. There will be no competition for us. Our worth magnifies when we value others without judging them. If we can keep these principles at the door of our hearts, his blessings will continue to flow in our lives.

- How does this resonate with you?
- What do your love and faithfulness look like today?
- How can you align them with his will?

_____

_____

Dear lord, great is thy faithfulness. I am forever grateful for your favor and countless blessings. May my life pour into others as you pour into mine. In Jesus' name, Amen.

Subscribe to www.samariakelly.com for more inspirational products.

Perfectly Flawed: Your 30-Day Devotional Guide on How to Accept and Love You – Seeing You Through His Eyes

DAY TWENTY
WEAKNESS = STRENGTH

- - - ·

But he said to me, "My grace is sufficient for you, for my power is made perfect in weakness." Therefore, I will boast all the more gladly of my weaknesses, so that the power of Christ may rest upon me. For the sake of Christ, then, I am content with weaknesses, insults, hardships, persecutions, and calamities. For when I am weak, then I am strong. 2 Corinthians 12:9-10 (ESV)

When we rid ourselves of pride and admit we are weak, we allow him to be God and make us strong. Knowing that we cannot do anything without him brings more glory and adoration to him and brings profound recognition to his power. Therefore, we should be at peace with our shortcomings and insecurities, for it is in these moments and circumstances that our Lord and Savior can exercise his mighty power and strength.

He adores this humbleness that allows him to show himself off. He loves it so much that he makes grace readily available to us. So embrace your authentic self with all that it brings, for your strength builds from it while you magnify his power. It's fine to not be fine. It's ok to not know it all. This is when God can be our all, and it's in these most vulnerable times that he truly receives the intimacy he desires from us.

- What are your convictions?
- How do you see your weaknesses?
- Do you allow God to be the source of your strength?
- Who do you lean on?

_____

_____

Dear God, I come to you with an open heart as humbly as I know how, asking you to give me strength in those areas that I am weak. Thank you for helping me realize that my shortcomings are a part of what makes me who I am and that they give me the opportunity to allow you to be God over my life. In Jesus' name, Amen.

Perfectly Flawed: Your 30-Day Devotional Guide on How to Accept and Love You — Seeing You Through His Eyes

DAY TWENTY ONE
BE HIS EXAMPLE

A new commandment I give to you, that you love one another: just as I have loved you, you also are to love one another. By this, all people will know that you are my disciples, if you have a love for one another.
John 13:34-35 (ESV)

When we love selflessly, we are acting as a present example of Christ. He instructs us to love each other beyond what we are naturally capable of doing. He wants us to love each other just as we love ourselves, and, even more so, just as He has loved us. If he can love us despite all that we have committed against him, then we, his followers, should be able to give love regardless of fault, debt, or disparity of person.

When we go against all expectations of those around us, it places us in a league of our own and classifies us as His very own. Everyone of every creed, of every seed and breed, will know love because God is love. Then we will know that we love correctly as He does.

- How are you representing love?
- Do you look like Christ?
- What can you do to look more like him?

_____

_____

Dear Lord, I appreciate your unfailing love for me. Thank you for loving me despite my faults. Help me love correctly, Oh Lord. Forgive me for those things I have done that have been without love. Continue to order my steps, Oh Lord. In Jesus' name, Amen.

Subscribe to www.samariakelly.com for more inspirational products.

Perfectly Flawed: Your 30-Day Devotional Guide on How to Accept and Love You – Seeing You Through His Eyes

DAY TWENTY-TWO
CHOSEN MEMBER

- - - - - - - - - - ● ● ● ● ● ● ● ● ● ● ● ● ● ● ● ● - - - - ·

But as it is, God arranged the members in the body, each one of them, as he chose. If all were a single member, where would the body be? As it is, there are many parts, yet one body. 1 Corinthians 12 18:20 (ESV)

There are many pieces to your being that are uniquely shaped and constructed to fit in its respective place. Only he knows the purpose behind each one. Since his judgment is never questionable and he operates in perfection always, we should have faith in his decision. We may not understand it completely, but it is not for us to understand everything anyway. We are to trust the one who created us. Even more, each of us are an important part of the body of Christ. No one is of less importance than the other. Just think about if the whole body was just a hand--how would we see, hear, feel, or speak? Or if the body was just an eye? We could only see but nothing else. Just imagine seeing your favorite dessert but being incapable of touching it, smelling it, or eating it.

We have to have respect for all the parts of our whole, for each part of us has an important task and is appropriate to us. We have to trust in him, believe in ourselves, our gifts, and not get dismayed or discouraged because we look different, walk a certain way, or talk a specific way. You are only competing with yourself if you do this. How awkward to imagine that!

- Are we battling with ourselves and our bodies?
- What can we do to change those feelings?

Dear Lord, you make all things perfect. Everything you created is magnificent, and I adore your craftsmanship and your designing me for a special purpose. I am confident that I am nothing short of amazing because of you. In Jesus' name, Amen.

Subscribe to www.samariakelly.com for more inspirational products.

Perfectly Flawed: Your 30-Day Devotional Guide on How to Accept and Love You – Seeing You Through His Eyes

Subscribe to www.samariakelly.com for more inspirational products.

DAY TWENTY-THREE
LET LOVE LIVE

No one has ever seen God; if we love one another, God abides in us and his love is perfected in us.
1 John 4:12 (ESV)

We understand that when we allow love to flow from our lives into other's lives that we are allowing them to meet God, to experience his presence. How powerful! He lives in us, so we give him to others when we give love. This is so important because, without love, God is not clearly seen. When we can't express and spread love, how are we going to affect someone's life? We must permit love in every situation.

We could be the only connection or interaction someone has with God. We could be the only hope they have to continue on and not give up. It has to be a selfless act to prevail. We must also keep in mind that we have all fallen short, so don't let judgment get in the way. Then love can operate in its perfection.

Subscribe to www.samariakelly.com for more inspirational products.

Perfectly Flawed: Your 30-Day Devotional Guide on
How to Accept and Love You – Seeing You Through His
Eyes

- Are you perfected in love?
- What are some of your current challenges?
- Are you allowing God to abide in you?

_____

_____

Dear Heavenly Father, I am nothing without you. In you I have my being, and I desire more of you. Help me prove myself acceptable and continue to allow your love to flow through my daily works. In Jesus' name, Amen.

Perfectly Flawed: Your 30-Day Devotional Guide on
How to Accept and Love You – Seeing You Through His
Eyes

Subscribe to www.samariakelly.com for more
inspirational products.

DAY TWENTY FOUR
PURPOSEFUL

- -

And I am sure of this, that he who began a good work in you will bring it to completion at the day of Jesus Christ. Philippians 1:6 (ESV)

Many times we get discouraged when we fail or don't meet the expectations of others. We lose confidence, second guess ourselves, or start having thoughts of not being good enough. Sometimes we even believe success is unattainable for us. When we decide to put all of our trust in God and not man (and stop aiming to prove ourselves and impress those around us), then we become winners, even when we fail. God will do what he said he is going to do in our lives. His plans for us will prosper in their respective season.

Nothing can stop us. Whatever he has for us will come to pass until he says it is complete. He is the author and finisher of our faith. He makes us accomplished, and the gifts he has given us are anointed and appointed in perfection.

Subscribe to www.samariakelly.com for more inspirational products.

- Are we confident in who we are and whose we are?
- Are we allowing the opinions of others to keep us from reaching our full potential?
- What do we need to change?

_____

_____

Dear God, I know I am a winner because I come from a winner. I can do all things through Christ who strengthens me. Everything I am is satisfactory because you said so, and it belongs to you. I am confident in who I am because I am from the best. I was born victorious. In Jesus' name, Amen.

Perfectly Flawed: Your 30-Day Devotional Guide on How to Accept and Love You – Seeing You Through His Eyes

DAY TWENTY-FIVE
NO APPROVAL NEEDED

*And God saw everything that he had made and
behold, it was **very** good. And there was evening,
and there was morning, the sixth day.* Genesis 1:31
(ESV)

God validates us, he gave us the stamp of
approval the moment he looked at us after he
completed us. It was an exaggerated satisfaction.
Talk about maximum security! This is all the
acceptance we need to feel confident of our very
selves. No one and nothing can alter this. God
makes no mistakes. He doesn't operate in confusion.
He was very sure that what he made was what he
desired, and it was very pleasing to him.

When we arrive in a moment of uncertainty
or we allow thoughts to discredit our capabilities
and our value, we must reflect on who gave us our
value. This is when we remain unstoppable and able
to reach our greatest achievement. We should

always keep in the back of our minds who it is that has proven us worthy and qualified.

- Do you feel good enough?
- Do you trust in those gifts that God has given you?
- Have you allowed the opinions of others to manifest in your life?
- If so, what can you do to reverse those thoughts and feelings to align with the truth?

_____

_____

Dear God, you deserve all the honor and glory! I am grateful that you chose me and you saw me worthy of love and life. I don't take this for granted for one second. Thank you for seeing the best in me, even at my worst. I speak against any thoughts of self-doubt or low self-worth. In Jesus' name, Amen.

Subscribe to www.samariakelly.com for more inspirational products.

Perfectly Flawed: Your 30-Day Devotional Guide on How to Accept and Love You — Seeing You Through His Eyes

Subscribe to www.samariakelly.com for more inspirational products.

DAY TWENTY-SIX
WE ARE BECAUSE OF HIM

- - - - - - - - - - ● ● ● ● ● ● ● ● ● - - - - - - -

The God who made the world and everything in it, being Lord of heaven and earth, does not live in temples made by man, nor is he served by human hands, as though he needed anything since he gives to all mankind life and breath and everything. And he made from one man every nation of mankind to live on all the face of the earth, having determined allotted periods and the boundaries of their dwelling place, that they should seek God, hoping they might feel their way toward him and find him. Yet he is close to each one of us, for in him, we live and move and have our being; as even some of your poets have said, "For we are indeed his offspring." Acts 17:24-28 (ESV)

We have given nothing to our Lord who made us, but he gave us everything. It brings Him honor when we are true to who we are and who we come from without fear. He has given us everything we will ever need and desire, from our essential breath to our dwelling place to our unveiling face. God made every nation in the world from one man. God places us when and where he wants us, hoping we will seek him first to allow him to be fully present and able to be who he is.

We get so distracted with the things of our natural realm of living that we unintentionally place him last instead of first. I'm guilty of this. He allows us to go through tests, trials, moments of despair, shame, guilt, and doubt so that we become humble enough to know that we need him and cannot do anything without him. It is not to discourage us, and it does not change our value, rather it is only to bring him to the forefront and remind us who is in control.

- Do you know who is the head of your life?
- Are you allowing God to direct your path?
- Are you giving credit where it is due and showing humility?

_____

_____

Perfectly Flawed: Your 30-Day Devotional Guide on How to Accept and Love You – Seeing You Through His Eyes

Dear Lord, I thank you for being God and the head of my life. Help me keep my mind stayed on you and to keep you first in all I do. In Jesus' name, Amen.

Perfectly Flawed: Your 30-Day Devotional Guide on
How to Accept and Love You – Seeing You Through His
Eyes

Subscribe to www.samariakelly.com for more
inspirational products.

DAY TWENTY-SEVEN
THE DIVINE

- - - - - - - ● ● ● ● ● ● ● ● ● ● ● ● ● ● - - - - - -

He is the image of the invisible God, the firstborn of all creation. For by him all things were created, in heaven and on earth, visible and invisible, whether thrones or dominions or rulers or authorities—all things were created through him and for him.
Colossians 1:15-16 (ESV)

If he has given us something to give back to him, wouldn't we say that it was of excellent quality? He wouldn't have insured us with anything that he didn't see as beyond perfection or impressive enough to represent him and receive it with gladness. We should have comfort in knowing we don't have to prove ourselves and try so hard to be ourselves. If we choose to put all of our trust in our Lord and we trust in his works and what he has put within us, we will have all the confidence we will ever need to pursue our calling and reach our destiny.

He equipped us as instruments to be used for him. Everything we can see and cannot see; great and small, black and white, rich or poor, exists to bring praise to him. So those gifts that we have hidden within our souls are to shine through and glorify him and his kingdom.

- Are you purpose-driven to win?
- Do you understand your purpose and who is your Director?
- Are you using your gifts to uplift his kingdom?

_____

_____

Dear Heavenly Father, I praise you for giving me gifts that are special and perfect for me. I will use those gifts as instruments of praise to you, for everything you have given me belongs to you and for your glory. In Jesus' name, Amen.

Subscribe to www.samariakelly.com for more inspirational products.

Perfectly Flawed: Your 30-Day Devotional Guide on How to Accept and Love You – Seeing You Through His Eyes

Subscribe to www.samariakelly.com for more inspirational products.

DAY TWENTY-EIGHT
D.N.A

· · · · · · · · · ● ◉ ◉ ◉ ◉ ● · · · · · ·

*The Lord possessed me at the beginning of his work,
the first of his acts of old. Ages ago I was set up, at
the first, before the beginning of the earth.*
Proverbs 8:22-23 (ESV)

God already had our layout at the beginning
of the world. I'm envisioning a silhouette of some
sort waiting for his signal of life, prior to any idea
of land, with his tools, in order to manifest our
existence in them. God used himself as the base, the
core of our makeup. He was the blueprint! We are
not here by default. We were his first acts before a
clock could tick. We are his literal first loves.
He set us up to win before we were winners! Our
Victory happened long before there was even a
fight. It's in our D.N.A.: Divine Natural Ability!
We are of him and he is of us. We can
achieve anything because our power and strength
comes directly from him. We get in our own way.

Perfectly Flawed: Your 30-Day Devotional Guide on How to Accept and Love You – Seeing You Through His Eyes

We must remain confident in our D.N.A. or our Divine Natural Ability to walk in authority.

- Do you know who you are?
- Do you feel like a divine winner right now?
- What are your current struggles?

_____

_____

Dear Lord, you are wonderful. There will never be enough words to describe how great you are. I'm blessed to be yours. Nothing is impossible for me. I am more than a conqueror. In Jesus' name, Amen.

Subscribe to www.samariakelly.com for more inspirational products.

Perfectly Flawed: Your 30-Day Devotional Guide on
How to Accept and Love You – Seeing You Through His
Eyes

Subscribe to www.samariakelly.com for more
inspirational products.

DAY TWENTY-NINE
GOOD ENOUGH

- - - - - - - - - - ◦ ◦ ◦ ◦ ◉ ◉ ◉ ◉ ◦ ◦ ◦ ◦ - - - - - - - -

For everything God created is good, and nothing is to be rejected if it is received with thanksgiving.
1 Timothy 4:4 (NIV)

We are remarkable! He said it right here, so we can get rid of all the misconceptions of society, ignore our fellow naysayers, and reject the false claims made by the enemy. He said everything he created was good. If you believe God made you, then you are good. He has repeated this over three times, so it is of great importance and should stick to our hearts. Even if our mind wanders from this foundation, it will find its way back to the truth.

No one has the authority to reject what God has accepted. Since he chose it and accepted it as satisfying, we should receive it all with a heart of gratitude. We should not look for fault, scan for blemishes, or analyze for errors. We must welcome everything that God created with open arms and be thankful.

Subscribe to www.samariakelly.com for more inspirational products.

- Are you still wrestling with feelings of self-doubt?
- What are your exact convictions?
- What will it take to gain the confidence necessary for your breakthrough?

_____

_____

Dear Lord, I serve you with gladness! Thank you for your amazing power and love. Thank you for making me in your likeness and no less than anyone, an original created by your loving desires. In Jesus' name, Amen.

Subscribe to www.samariakelly.com for more inspirational products.

Perfectly Flawed: Your 30-Day Devotional Guide on How to Accept and Love You – Seeing You Through His Eyes

DAY THIRTY
GOD ABIDES WITH LOVE

So we have come to know and to believe the love that God has for us. God is love, and whoever abides in love abides in God, and God abides in him. 1 John 4:16 (ESV)

We are now officially wise in love and believe the love that God has for us. We can receive it and share it. This has become second nature. It will now happen without hesitation. It is always present; the word abides means to stay, live, and remain. We indeed have love living in us, and if love is within us, God is within us because both are one. We must still allow this to be possible. God is free, which means love is free. We must freely choose them.

When we decide to remain in love, which means remain in God, we will see changes in the way we walk, talk, act, and treat others. For what is in us must come out in our everyday walk. We will transform our entire outlook on life. We can say love brought us to victory! Hello, victory. Goodbye, defeat! Challenges will no longer be challenges. They will be tests that turn into testimonies, trials will be triumphs, and our stresses will become blessings.

- Reflect on this journey.
- Reflect on how you feel at this moment.
- What are your thoughts on this experience?

_____

_____

Dear Lord, please continue to guide me on this journey of life. Let love be the center of everything that I do in my daily walk. Let me be a worthy example of your glory and represent you with excellence. I know if I seek you first and keep you first that everything else will fall in place. Thank you for loving me and choosing me to be one of yours. In Jesus' name, Amen.

Subscribe to www.samariakelly.com for more inspirational products.

Perfectly Flawed: Your 30-Day Devotional Guide on How to Accept and Love You – Seeing You Through His Eyes

A SPECIAL NOTE FOR YOU

Congratulations, you have just unlocked a world of unlimited possibilities. The enemy is now afraid of you. Your driver's license is no longer your primary form of identification. You know who you are and your worth, and you have God with you. I hope you feel like a butterfly who just learned how to spread its wings and fly, and now it can go wherever it pleases. There are no more barriers or any force of captivity preventing it from elevating and reaching its destiny. This is exactly how I felt the moment I realized my value and who was my source of strength and power.

A prayer for you from *Ephesians 3:16-19 (NIV):*

"I pray that out of his glorious riches he may strengthen you with power through his Spirit in your inner being, so that Christ may dwell in your hearts through faith. And I pray that you, being rooted and established in love, may have power, together with

Subscribe to www.samariakelly.com for more inspirational products.

all the Lord's holy people, to grasp how wide and long and high and deep is the love of Christ, and to know this love that surpasses knowledge --that you may be filled to the measure of all the fullness of God."

Perfectly Flawed: Your 30-Day Devotional Guide on How to Accept and Love You – Seeing You Through His Eyes

Subscribe to www.samariakelly.com for more inspirational products.

THANK YOU

Thank you for taking the time to read my devotional guide. I'd love to hear about your thoughts and experiences. Please leave a review on Amazon @bit.ly/AuthorSamariaKelly or contact me directly @www.samariakelly.com. This is also where you can subscribe to keep up with my latest releases, receive first-hand alerts on discounts and giveaways, and gain access to my other inspirational products.

Until next time, be blessed,

Samaria Kelly

Subscribe to www.samariakelly.com for more inspirational products.

Perfectly Flawed: Your 30-Day Devotional Guide on
How to Accept and Love You – Seeing You Through His
Eyes

Subscribe to www.samariakelly.com for more
inspirational products.

www.ingramcontent.com/pod-product-compliance
Lightning Source LLC
Chambersburg PA
CBHW030109070426
42448CB00036B/584